Wind-down Activities

Alice James, Lara Bryan
and Darran Stobbart

Illustrated by
**Manu Montoya
and Ada Crowe**

Designed by
Tilly Kitching

With expert advice from
Dr. Angharad Rudkin

Wind-down time

Sometimes you need to think fast and zoom around.
Other times you need to wind down and take things slow.
This book is full of things to do during those calm times,
to give your brain the chance to settle and reset.

Just flip through
the book and pick
an activity that
takes your fancy.

Every activity is
designed to help
you chill out.

You can fill in any of the
drawings in this book
that you want to.

Things to look out for

You'll spot this pattern on pages that tell you all about the SCIENCE of winding down – from sleep, to showers, to the power of hugs.

To help you really switch off and just focus on what you're doing, there are links to music dotted throughout the book. Listen to them while you fill things in.

Look out for this symbol. If you scan it with the camera on a smartphone or tablet, it will take you to a piece of music.

USBORNE QUICKLINKS

For links to the music chosen for this book and websites with even more activities, visit **usborne.com/Quicklinks** and type in the title of this book.

Please follow the online safety guidelines at Usborne Quicklinks. Children should be supervised online.

As the sun sets, the twilight world appears.
Imagine you're looking through these binoculars
at a woodland at dusk. What can you spot?

A comfy tent

Pale, fluttering moths

These are all
NOCTURNAL animals.
They come out at
night when it's
dusky and dark.

A firefly – a type of
beetle with a body that
lights up in the dark.

Circling crows. At the end of the day, birds are getting ready to sleep.

You could do this in real life too. At dusk, sit quietly and look outside. What can you spot?

An owl waiting patiently on a branch

A skulking cat

The hint of the moon, starting to appear

The bright, shining eyes of a creature in a tree

Listen along as you fill in the page.

You don't need to fill it all in.
Just do what you'd like to, and
come back another time.

Focus on breathing in...
...and out. Imagine your
breath is the wind blowing
these balloons along.

The science of...
slowing down

If you're feeling anxious or tense, you can use a tool called

MINDFULNESS

to slow everything down.

Being mindful uses all of your senses to be present in the here and now.

It relaxes your body and slows your heart...

...as well as calming your thoughts and worries.

When you're feeling a bit overwhelmed, focus on the things you can...

...hear

...feel

...see

...smell

Take a moment to focus on getting your pencil to the middle of this labyrinth. There's only one way through a labyrinth, so you can't get lost.

Cut and stick things onto the owl's wings to create a magnificent swoop of feathers.

Cut ovals out of old patterned paper or magazines.

Tear small strips of newspaper.

Imagine this is your very own wind-down chest, full of calming tools to help you relax. Write or draw anything you can think of – real or imaginary.

Here are some ideas to get you started.

A shield that you can use to block worries

A magic harp that can play you soothing music all by itself

An extra comfy cushion that helps you get to sleep

Blow inky bubbles

Put a squirt of liquid paint, a squirt of dishwashing liquid and a splash of water in a small cup or tub.

Mix it up with a straw. Then blow gently through the straw until bubbles appear and rise in the tub.

Place a piece of paper face-down on top of the tub, to leave painty bubbles on the page. Then, let it dry.

When the paper has dried, cut out the bubble prints and stick them here.

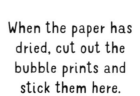

Draw bubbles
Add more bubbles
to fill the space.

Doodle bubbles
Doodle patterns and
shapes inside these
bubbles here.

Escaping into a made-up world is a great way to wind down and distract yourself from your surroundings. Pick a story starter that sparks your imagination and start writing...

You spot an unusual item on a shop shelf.
What do you do?

What does this key open?

Grow a mertail and follow me! There are dolphins to dive with, seaweed forests to explore and a wise old turtle to meet.

Move to Moontown!

Be part of the first community in space.

Where are these footsteps going and who made them?

If you're inspired, keep writing on another piece of paper.

Scan this QR code, or listen to some music you particularly like.

How does the music make you feel?
What words come to mind?
Write them in the spaces on this page.

Really focus on the music.
What instruments can you hear? Is it fast or slow?
Is it happy or sad?

This QR code links to another piece of music. Do different songs make you think of different things? Compare how the pieces of music make you feel.

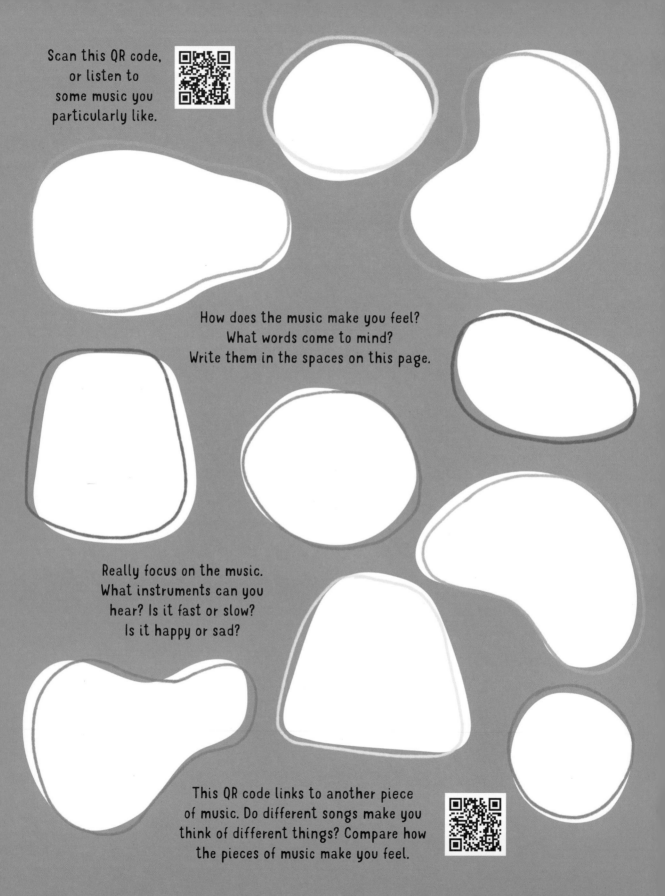

Follow these lines and carry them on.
Let them slide and swoop all over the page
along to the music you're listening to.

Use different pens
or pencils for
each tune.

Follow these instructions to make some ooey, gooey stuff. Some people call it oobleck. Relax as you squash and squeeze it in your hands.

You will need

A bowl
80g (3oz) cornflour
(known as cornstarch in the US)
60ml (1/2 cup) water
A spoon
Food dye (optional)

Put the cornflour in a bowl.

Slowly stir in the water.

If it's dry and crumbly, add a little more water. If it's wet and drippy, add more cornflour.

You could add a drop of food dye too.

Now it's time to play with it. Keep it in the bowl, or put it on a tray. Try each of these things – what happens?

Push your finger into it slooooowly.

Stir it slowly.

Pour it into another bowl.

Oobleck is something scientists call a non-Newtonian fluid. Sometimes it acts like a drippy liquid, and sometimes it acts like a hard solid.

Punch it gently.

Stir it fast!

Try to hold it in your hands over a bowl or tray.

Squiggle it with a fork.

Squeeze it through your fingers.

The science of...
smells

For thousands of years, people have known
that some smells can be really

SOOOOOOOOOOOTHING.

When you smell something nice, it triggers a message that
gets sent to your brain and helps you to relax.

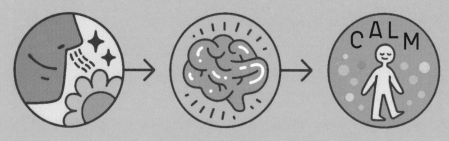

Scientists call this the

OLFACTORY RESPONSE.

Lavender

For example, the
herbs LAVENDER and
ROSEMARY have been
used for centuries to
help people sleep.

Rosemary

Try sniffing a wide range of things.
See how each one makes you feel. Use the space below
to keep track of the smells you find the most calming.

Smell	How did it make you feel?
Minty toothpaste	
Grass	
Clean laundry	
A soft toy	
Vanilla ice cream	

Fill these pages with doodles. They can be big or small, rough or neat... Just fill ALL the space.

You could doodle pictures...

...patterns

...shapes

...words.

HAPPY

Scan here to listen
as you doodle.

Doodling can help
your brain focus on
other tasks.

Calming down your BODY sends messages straight to your brain to calm it down TOO. Try these four ways of shaking out your body and getting it to relax.

Move

Just MOVE!

Flap your arms. Shake out all the pent-up energy in your hands and arms.

Run up some stairs or on the spot.

Dance around.

Moving around and being active releases happy, calming chemicals called ENDORPHINS in your brain.

Really breathe

One of the BEST things you can do to wind down is to BREATHE.

Breathe in while you count to three...

...and out while you count to three.

Deep breaths slow your heart down and help your muscles relax. Your WHOLE body and brain feel calmer.

Streeeetch

Stretch UP to
the sky.

Stretching is GOOD.
Think about how
each part of your
body is feeling as
you stretch it out.

REACH out
to the sides.

Fold DOWN
to the floor.

Mini massage

A mini massage can help you squeeze out any stressed
feelings that you're holding in your body.

Massage your head with
your fingertips, as if you're
rubbing in shampoo.

Rub little circles on your
shoulders and neck.

Relax and unwind with some music, as you fill the patterns on this page. Choose small sections at a time - you don't need to finish it all at once, or finish it at all.

Often, when you wake up, your head is still full
of parts of a dream you've just been having.
Keep this book by your bed and write down
anything you remember as soon as you wake up.

Capture what's
on your mind
before the dream
fades away.

Date:
Dream:

Taking a moment to jot down thoughts can be a quiet, gentle way to start the day.

Date:
Dream:

Date:
Dream:

Dreams probably help you sort through information and feelings from the day – but scientists don't know for sure why we have them.

Date:
Dream:

If you have a bad dream, it sometimes helps to write it down and invent a happy ending.

Date:
Dream:

The melody of the song *Let it be* came to Beatles musician, Paul McCartney, in a dream.

From the pitter patter of rain, to the soft sighing of ocean waves, soothing sounds can be found everywhere. Here are some you can make yourself.

Fill three or four drinking glasses with different amounts of water.

Tap the rim of each glass with a pencil.

How does the amount of water in each glass change the sound you make?

Make some melodies by hitting the glasses in different combinations.

Create rhythms using just your body. A rhythm is a repeated, varied pattern of sounds. Build one like this...

Start by clapping your hands.

Add in some foot stomps in between claps.

Add some clicks between the claps too.

CLAP
CLAP

STOMP
SMACK

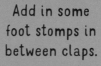

CLICK
CLICK

Make some bottle maracas by half-filling some old plastic bottles with rice, dried lentils or pasta.

Screw the lids back onto each bottle tightly.

Try different sized bottles. Do they make different sounds?

What happens to the sound if you change how much rice or pasta the bottle contains?

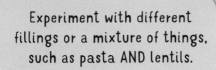

Experiment with different fillings or a mixture of things, such as pasta AND lentils.

Now shake your bottle maracas.

Scan this QR code to hear some music you can shake your maracas to.

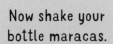

The science of...
hugs

Brain scientists have shown that a big

HUG

is a great way to wind down.

Hugs cause your brain to release a chemical called OXYTOCIN.

Oxytocin calms down stressful feelings, and slows your heart rate.

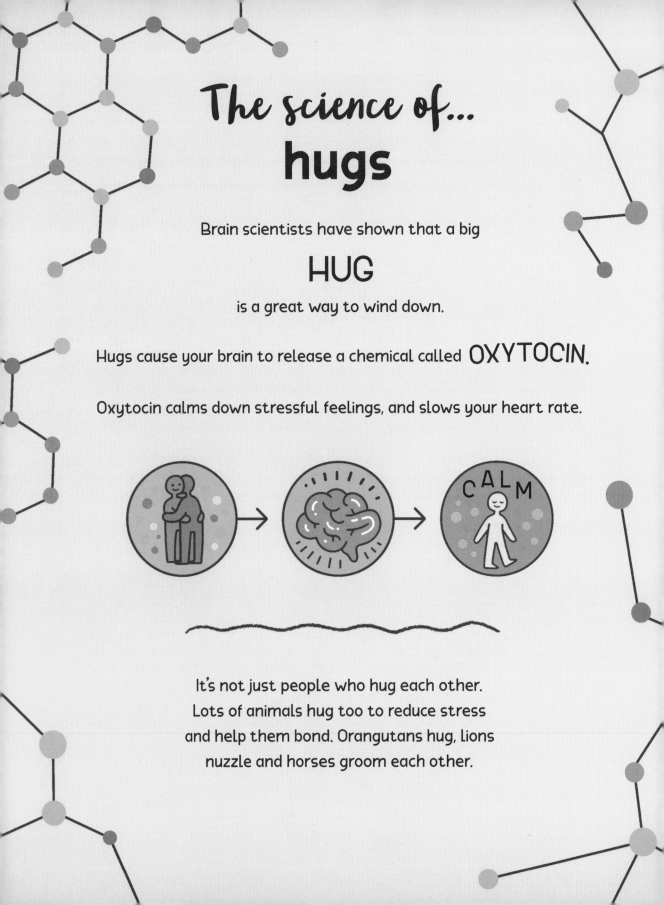

It's not just people who hug each other.
Lots of animals hug too to reduce stress
and help them bond. Orangutans hug, lions
nuzzle and horses groom each other.

Grab a soft toy, and spend a moment wrapped up in a hug. If you prefer, you could hug someone in your family or a friend instead.

What does the soft toy smell like?

What sounds can you hear drifting in the background?

How does the fabric of your soft toy feel against your skin?

If you have a pet, such as a cat or a dog, you could try giving them a hug if they're happy with it.

How do you feel after your cuddle? Does your body feel calmer?

Use this space to draw a map of a
fantasy island to get lost in.

Add places for
people to live.

Island View
Lighthouse

Hupperdook Town

Are there any
lakes or rivers?

You could take inspiration
from places that you know,
or come up with something
completely new.

Use this space to
invent a name for
your island.

Add natural features –
trees, mountains
and volcanoes.

Dragon's Breath Volcano

The Veridian Woods

Come up with names for
any towns, forests or other
landmarks, and add them
to the map.

All sorts of creatures build nests to live and sleep in. A good nest is a secure and comfy space, where animals feel safe. Design your own nest on the next page, taking inspiration from the real animals here.

Gentoo penguins build piles of stones to nest on, to keep themselves off the chilly ground.

Blue tits line their tiny nests with soft feathers and moss.

Chipmunks camouflage the entrance to their underground dens so nothing can find them.

Rabbits burrow underground in a nest called a warren. There are different "rooms" and tunnels inside.

SLEEP

FOOD

You could build your nest in real life too. Here are some ideas for things you could use...

Cushions

Blankets

String

Chairs as side supports

Towels

Bed sheets

The underneath of a table

Big cardboard boxes

String of lights

This cabinet is in desperate need of some sorting out. Save the day by restoring order.

Correct the labels on this collection of small treasures by unscrambling the letters.

Can you write the missing titles on these book spines? The books need to be arranged by alphabetical order, from top to bottom.

WORLD OF DINOSAURS
TOP 100 INVENTIONS
Adventures of Puss in Boots
ENGLISH DICTIONARY
My First Cookbook

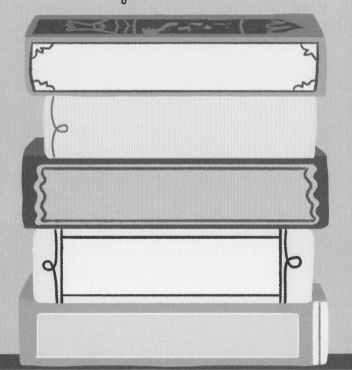

ROUF-ELAF VRCLOE

....

NSAW TREFAHE

....

BRAC CERPIN

....

Draw markings on the blank marbles so they follow the pattern.

These pictures show the same scene just a couple of minutes apart.
Can you spot the differences?

2:25pm

2:30pm

2:34pm

Draw the missing shells, so that each
row, column and four-square box has a
shell of each shape.

If you've enjoyed these
puzzles, you might find
sorting things in real life
satisfying too.

Follow these steps to make your very own wind-down team, to give you a reassuring boost whenever you need it.

You will need   A pencil   A piece of paper   Scissors

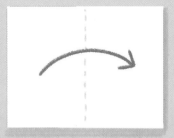

1 Fold your piece of paper in half, short edge to short edge.

2 Fold it in half the same way again.

3 Cut the piece of paper in half, like this.

4 Draw the outline of a person on the top layer.

You could copy this one, or draw it HOWEVER you like. Just make sure the arms stretch to the very edges of the paper.

5 Now cut around your person. Make sure you don't cut through the hands!

6 Unfold and see your wind-down team appear.

The more times you fold your piece of paper, the longer your chain of people will be.

Decorate them however you like.

Often it's easier to be kind and encouraging to other people than to yourself. Imagine one of your paper people needed calming down. What would you tell them?

Breeeeeathe

Find somewhere comfy and sit as quietly as you can. What can you hear? Write, doodle or draw the sounds here. The more you try listening, the better you get at really hearing stuff.

A plane flying past, high above you

A pigeon cooing

A car

Purrrrrrr

A purring cat

You could listen to the soundscape here instead. What sounds can you pick out?

Close your eyes and listen
again. When you block off
one of your senses, your
other ones work harder.
Can you hear more with
your eyes closed?

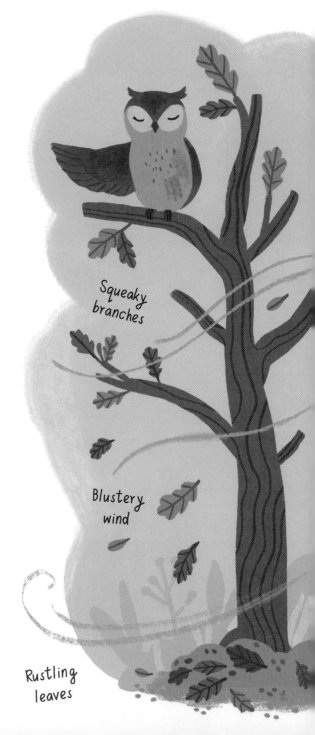

Squeaky
branches

Blustery
wind

Rustling
leaves

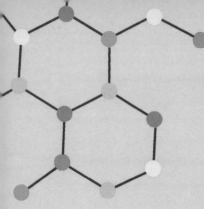

The science of...
showers

A warm shower or bath sends a message to your body to calm down.

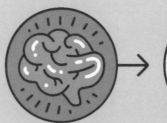 

Hot water heats up your skin. Then, as you cool down afterwards, your body *reallllly relaxes.*

Steamy air in a bathroom can also help you breathe big, deep breaths. This is great for your body and brain.

Japanese hot spring

In Japan, baths at home, in hot springs, or in public baths, are thought to help your body, mind and soul, as well as making you clean.

Next time you're in a shower or bath, have a think about...

The smell of
your soap

The feel of the warm
water and foam

The sound of splishing
and sploshing

Design your perfect bath

Use the space here to design the best bath you can imagine.
You can draw it or write about it. What shape is the tub?
How big is it? Is it bubbly? What does it smell like?

My perfect bathtub
would be shaped like
a pirate ship and full
of big strawberry-
scented bubbles.

Escape into an adventure where you're the main character.

First things first, decide where your adventure will be set.
You can use one of the suggestions here or make up one of your own.

How about a fantasy realm?

A futuristic city?

An icy tundra?

Let your imagination go wild!

Sketch or describe your setting below.

Now it's time to design your outfit. The clothes and equipment you'll need will depend on where you're adventuring.

What do you want to call yourself? It could be your own name, or you could make one up.

....

Do you need any headgear? Maybe a knight's helmet? Or some flying goggles?

What kind of equipment might you need to bring with you?

It's important to have sensible footwear. Will you need flippers on your adventure?

Or maybe shoes with springs in them to help you jump?

Once you've created your main character, you could write a story about your adventures on another sheet of paper.

As you fill the scene, listen to this Venetian music.

Imagine the sound of babbling water and the breeze drifting through the peaceful streets.

You can come back to this
page again and again.

Getting thoughts out of your head and onto paper can help you feel calmer and take pressure off your brain. With a clear head you're more likely to have a good night's sleep.

Use these little pieces of paper to write or draw out any thoughts, worries or lists in your head.

On a clear, cloudless night, look up at the night sky and jot down what you can see. It's a great way to unwind before bed as your brain responds to darkness by making you feel sleepy.

How many stars you can spot? On a clear night, if you could look in ALL directions from Earth, you'd see over 9,000 stars.

The Moon looks bright because it reflects the light of the Sun.

The brightest star visible from Earth is called Sirius, which means "glowing" in ancient Greek.

You can tell planets apart from stars because stars twinkle and planets don't.

A light that's flashing isn't a star, it's a plane.

Mars has a reddish glow.

It's easier to do this activity in the countryside, where it's darker. But on cloudless nights city skies can be starry too.

If you're looking for a while, you might spot a white streak of light. This is a shooting star – a piece of space rock burning brightly as it enters Earth's atmosphere.

Early stargazers grouped stars into pictures and patterns called constellations.

Can you guess what pictures these constellations represent, by matching them to their name in the list below?

Great Bear
Scorpion
Orion the Hunter

Cetus

This constellation is named after an ancient Greek sea monster. It's sometimes called "the whale" in English.

Connect the stars here to create your own constellations. Scan this link for a piece of music inspired by the night sky.

Slotting the pieces of a jigsaw puzzle together is super satisfying. You could make your own with just a sheet of paper or cardboard, a pair of scissors and a pencil.

Use a page from a magazine, the back or front of a thin cardboard box or a drawing of your own.

1   First draw on shapes that will become the pieces of your puzzle.

You could draw wavy lines...

straight lines...

...or a simple grid.

2   Cut along the lines you've drawn.

3   Mix up the pieces, then try sliding them back into the right place.

Add missing lines on the blank pieces to finish off this puzzle picture.

The science of...
sleep

One of the most important things your brain needs is sleep. Sleeping gives your brain the time and space...

...to sort through what you've learned in the day

...to file away your memories

...and to get ready for another day.

All this keeps your brain healthy and helps you wake up feeling **realllllly rested.**

Sleep also helps you recover if you're ill.

Your brain encourages you to sleep by releasing a chemical known as

MELATONIN.

As it travels around your body, it helps your body to get ready to rest.

ZZZZZ

Here are some top tips to help bring on sleepiness.

Set up a snug bedtime routine so that your brain and body knows it's time to sleep and rest.

You could have a warm shower or bath to relax your body before getting into bed.

Try not to look at TV, phone or tablet screens before going to sleep. The light makes your brain feel more awake.

If your head is full of busy thoughts, write them down so you can forget about them until the morning.

Listen to a sleepy tune to help you drift off.

Once you're tucked up in bed with a cuddly toy if you want one, focus on something to help you relax. It could be making up a story or counting each breath as you breathe in... and out...

Night, night.

See if you can work out the answers to my quiz. Don't worry if you get stuck - turn the page for the answers.

1 How many eyelids do owls have?

(A) One

(B) Two - in case the first one gets tired.

(C) Three - one for blinking, one for sleeping and a transparent one to protect the eye.

2 Owls can turn their heads...

(A) ...45°

(B) ...270°

(C) ...360° - all the way around

3 Baby owls are born with just one...

(A) ...feather. It keeps them nice and warm.

(B) ...tooth, so they can tap their way out of their egg.

(C) ...eye open, in case the sun's too bright.

4 Why was Athena, the ancient Greek goddess of wisdom, often shown with an owl by her side?

(A) She adopted it as a pet after rescuing it from a hungry eagle.

(B) It showed that she could see the "whole truth" - as the owl helped her see all around.

(C) It kept her neck warm when she had forgotten her scarf at home.

5 What does the shade of an owl's eyes tell you?

(A) Where it lives. Owls with darker eyes live in colder place.

(B) How hungry it is. When they've just eaten, their eyes turn gold.

(C) When it likes to hunt. Owls with yellow eyes are daytime hunters. Owls with orange eyes are active at twilight. And dark-eyed owls usually fly at night.

6 Can you finish this saying inspired by William Shakespeare? "The foolish owl doth think it is wise, but the wise owl knows it is..."

(A) ...a fool.

(B) ...very wise indeed.

(C) ...ready to win a quiz show.

7 Which of these techniques is most likely to help YOU see in the dark?

(A) Wait – after twenty minutes or so in darkness, your eyes naturally adjust.

(B) Put on sunglasses – making it darker is sure to help.

(C) Harness your inner bat. Make noises and listen for the sounds bouncing off objects to reveal what's around you.

Answers

Puzzles

Jumbled labels: Four-leaf clover, Swan feather, Crab pincer

Books in alphabetical order:

Adventures of Puss in Boots

ENGLISH DICTIONARY

My First Cookbook

TOP 100 INVENTIONS

WORLD OF DINOSAURS

Constellations

Orange constellation:
Great Bear

Green constellation:
Orion the Hunter

Purple constellation:
Scorpion

Quiz

1. C, 2. B, 3. B, 4. B, 5. C, 6. A, 7. A

Design manager: Stephen Moncrieff   Additional design by Freya Harrison
American editor: Carrie Armstrong

First published in 2023 by Usborne Publishing Limited, 83-85 Saffron Hill, London EC1N 8RT, United Kingdom. usborne.com Copyright © 2023 Usborne Publishing Limited. The name Usborne and the Balloon logo are registered trade marks of Usborne Publishing Limited.
First published in America in 2023. Printed in China. UE.